D1291660

COMPLETE SPEAKER'S

AND

TOASTMASTER'S LIBRARY

Proverbs, Epigrams, Aphorisms,

Sayings, and Bon Mots

COMPLETE SPEAKER'S

AND

TOASTMASTER'S LIBRARY

Proverbs, Epigrams, Aphorisms, Sayings, and Bon Mots

by Jacob M. Braude

PRENTICE-HALL, INC.

Englewood Cliffs, N.J.

A

Ability

1. Behind an able man there are always other able men.

—Chinese

Absence

2. The absent are always in the wrong.

—English

3. Absence in love is like water on fire, a little quickens, but much extinguishes.

Accepting

4. Who accepts nothing has nothing to return.

—German

Accomplice

5. He who holds the ladder is as bad as the thief.

—German

6. He sins as much who holds the bag as he who puts into it.

—French

Accomplishment

7. The shortest answer is *doing* the thing.

8. Large trees give more shade than fruit.

Accuracy

9. Deviate an inch, lose a thousand miles.

—Chinese

Accusation

10. He who accuses too many accuses himself.

Achievement

11. Young people tell what they are doing, old people what they have done and fools what they wish to do.

—French

Acknowledgment

12. If you wish your merit to be known, acknowledge that of other people.

—Oriental

Action

13. You cannot do anything by doing nothing.

Adaptability

14. A wise man adapts himself to circumstances as water shapes itself to the vessel that contains it

—Chinese

Admiration

15. In some respects it is better to be admired by those with whom you live than to be loved by them, because admiration is more tolerant than love.

Alcohol

16. Let him who sins when drunk be punished when sober.

—Legal maxim

17. What soberness conceals
Drunkenness reveals.

Ambition

18. Where ambition ends happiness begins.

—Hungarian

19. By jumping at the stars you may fall in the mud.

20. Better to light one candle than to curse the darkness.

—Chinese

21. If begging should unfortunately be thy lot, knock at the large gates only.

—Arabian

22. He who sacrifices his conscience to ambition burns a picture to obtain the ashes.

—Chinese

Ancestors—Ancestry

23. They brag most of their ancestors who are unworthy of them.

—Danish

24. From our ancestors come our names, but from our virtues our honors.

Anecdote—Anecdotes

25. One personal anecdote of a man is worth a volume of biography.

Anger

26. The best answer to anger is silence.

—German

27. Anger is only one letter short of danger.

28. Steel loses much of its value when it loses its temper.

29. So long as a man is angry he cannot be in the right.

—Chinese

30. It is easier to swallow angry words than to have to eat them.

31. He is a fool who cannot be angry; but he is a wise man who will not.

32. He that is slow to anger is better than the mighty: and he that ruleth his spirit than he that taketh a city.

—*Proverbs* XVI, 32

Answer

33. The shortest answer is performing the request.

Anticipation

34. A danger foreseen is half avoided.

Appearances

35. If the beard were all, goats could preach.

—Danish

36. A red-nosed man may be a teetotaler, but will find no one to believe it.

—Chinese

Argument—Arguments

37. Fools, for arguments, use wagers.

38. Wise men argue causes, fools often decide them.

39. Argument seldom convinces anyone against his inclination.

40. Calmness in argument is a great advantage for he who lets another chafe, warms him at his fire.

41. Whoever fears to submit any question to the test of free discussion, loves his own opinion more than the truth.

42. Answer not a fool according to his folly, lest thou also be like unto him. Answer a fool according to his folly lest he be wise in his own conceit.

Armed Forces

43. The best soldiers are not warlike.

—Chinese

Associate—Associates

44. When a dove begins to associate with crows its feathers remain white but its heart grows black.

—German

Attire

45. Eat whatever thou likest, but dress as others do.

—Arabian

B

Bandwagon

46. Everyone pushes a falling fence.

—Chinese

Beauty

47. Beauty, unaccompanied by virtue, is as a flower without perfume.

—French

Begging

48. It is a beggar's pride that he is not a thief.

—Japanese

Betting

49. Betting is a fool's argument, but it's very convincing when you win.

Blame

50. A bad workman quarrels with his tools.

Boastfulness

51. He that boasts of his own knowledge proclaims his ignorance.

52. They who boast most, generally fail most, for deeds are silent.

53. He who prides himself upon wealth and honor hastens his own downfall.

54. It is harder to be poor without complaining than to be rich without boasting.

—Chinese

55. When a man boasts about what he'll do tomorrow we like to find out what he did yesterday.

Book—Books

56. A wicked book cannot repent.

57. A book that is shut is but a block.

58. A man is himself—plus the books he reads.

59. God deliver me from a man of one book.

60. A book is a garden carried in the pocket.

—Arabian

Borrowing

61. He who borrows sells his freedom.

—German

62. Beware of going security for thy friends; he who payeth another man's debts, seeketh his own decay.

Broad-Mindedness

63. The broad-minded see the truth in different religions; the narrow-minded see only the differences.

—Chinese

Brotherhood

64. At the narrow passage there is no brother and no friend.

—Arabian

65. You can't spell "brothers" without at the same time spelling "others."

Business

66. Hold back some goods for a thousand days and you will be sure to sell at a profit.

—Chinese

C

Capacity

67. Little pots soon run over.

—Dutch

Caution

68. When the cup is full, carry it even.

—Scotch

69. To a quick question, give a slow answer.

—Italian

70. Wait till it is night before saying it has been a fine day.

—French

71. Look before you leap, for snakes among sweet flowers do creep.

72. Find a man smart enough to beat the other fellow's game, and he's too smart to play it.

73. If one has to jump a stream and knows how wide it is, he will not jump. If he does not know how wide it is, he will jump, and six times out of ten he will make it.

—Persian

Censure

74. Let your pride pardon what your nature needs, the salutary censure of a friend.

Certainty

75. Better an egg today than a hen tomorrow.

—Italian

76. If you forsake a certainty and depend on an uncertainty, you will lose both the certainty and the uncertainty.

—Sanskrit

Chaos

77. Chaos results when the world changes faster than people.

Character

78. A crooked stick will have a crooked shadow.

79. Character, like a kettle, once mended, always requires repairs.

80.   A person shows what he is by what he does with what he has.

81.   You can tell what a man is by what he does when he hasn't anything to do.

Charity

82.   Charity sees the need; not the cause.

—German

Cheating

83.   He who purposely cheats his friend would cheat his God.

Cheerfulness

84.   Continual cheerfulness is a sign of wisdom.

—Irish

Child—Children

85.   If a man leaves little children behind him, it is as if he did not die.

—Moroccan

Child Guidance

86.   He who takes a child by the hand takes a mother by the heart.

—Danish

Christianity

87.   When the world is at its worst, Christians must be at their best.

Common Sense

88.   A handful of common sense is worth a bushel of learning.

89.   One pound of learning requires ten pounds of common sense to apply it.

—Persian

Companionship

90. He that lies with dogs rises with fleas.

Comparison

91. To compare is not to prove.

—French

Compliment—Complimentary

92. Of a compliment only a third is meant.

—Welsh

Compromise

93. Better bend than break.

—Scottish

Condonation

94. For the sake of one good action a hundred evil ones should be forgotten.

—Chinese

Confession

95. Confession is the first step to repentance.

—English

Confidence

96. The dog that licks ashes is not to be trusted with flour.

—Italian

Conflict

97. Nobody can live longer in peace than his neighbor pleases.

10

Conformity

98. Either do as your neighbors do, or move away.

—Moroccan

Conscience

99. When you have no observers be afraid of yourself.

100. There is a difference between him who does no misdeeds because of his own conscience and him who is kept from wrongdoing because of the presence of others.

Contentment

101. Do not anxiously hope for that which is not yet come; do not vainly regret what is already past.

—Chinese

Cooperation

102. One hand cannot applaud.

—Arabian

103. Help thy brother's boat across, and Lo! thine own has reached the shore.

—Hindu

Courage

104. Courage consists not so much in avoiding danger as in conquering it.

Courtesy

105. An excess of courtesy is discourtesy.

—Japanese

106. No man is too big to be courteous, but some are too little.

Covetousness

107. The pleasure of what we enjoy is lost by coveting more.

Cowardice

108. It is cowardly to fly from a living enemy or to abuse a dead one.

—Danish

109. It is better to be a coward for a minute than dead the rest of your life.

—Irish

110. Of two cowards, the one who finds the other out first has the advantage.

—Italian

Credit

111. Buying on trust is the way to pay double.

Crime—Punishment

112. He who profits by a crime, commits it.

113. He who spares the guilty threatens the innocent.

—Legal maxim

114. If you share your friend's crime, you make it your own.

—Latin

115. Stone walls do not a prison make nor iron bars a cage.

116. To violate the law is the same crime in the emperor as in the subject.

—Chinese

117. He who overlooks a crime, encourages the commission of another.

118. It is not the thief who is hanged, but one who was caught stealing.

—Czech

Criticism

119. Tall trees catch much wind.

120. If you stop every time a dog barks, your road will never end.

—Arabian

121. Most knocking is done by folks who don't know how to ring the bell.

122. Justly to discriminate, wisely to prescribe, and honestly to award, should be the aim of all criticism.

Cruelty

123. Find a cruel man and you see a coward.

Custom—Customs

124. To circumstances and custom, the law must yield.

D

Death

125. He waits long that waits for another man's death.

—Dutch

126. Good men must die, but death cannot kill their names.

127. When your foes die, let all resentment cease;
Make peace with death, and death shall give you
    peace!

—Greek

Debate

128. In all debates, let truth be thy aim, and endeavor to gain rather than expose thy opponent.

Debt—Debts

129. He is rich who owes nothing.

—Hungarian

130. He who promises runs into debt.

131. It is hard to pay for bread that has been eaten.

132. Debts are like children: the smaller they are the more noise they make.

—Spanish

133. He who wants Lent to seem short should contract a debt to be repaid at Easter.

—Italian

Debtor—Creditor

134. No man is impatient with his creditors.

135. Every time you lend money to a friend you have a tendency to damage his memory.

Deception

136. He is not deceived who knows himself to be deceived.

—Legal maxim

137. If a man deceive me once shame on him, if he deceive me twice shame on me.

Decision—Decisions

138. Necessity requires no decision.

Delay

139. Deliberation is not delaying.

140. Where duty is plain, delay is dangerous; where it is not, delay may be wise and safe.

Denial

141. He who denies all confesses all.

—Spanish

Depletion

142. Taking out without putting in soon comes to the bottom.

Depression

143. During a depression we lose our houses; during prosperity we lose our homes.

Despicability

144. A man must make himself despicable before he is despised by others.

—Chinese

Destiny

145. Destiny leads the willing but drags the unwilling.

Detection

146. No one can be caught in places he does not visit.

—Danish

Determination

147. Follow the river and you will find the sea.

—French

148.   To him who is determined it remains only to act.

—Italian

Diagnosis

149.   The first step toward cure is to know what the disease is.

—Latin

Diet

150.   Whatsoever was the father of disease, an ill diet was the mother.

Dignity

151.   It is only people of small moral stature who have to stand on their dignity.

Disappointment

152.   The most disappointed people in the world are those who get what is coming to them.

Discontent—Discontentment

153.   The root of discontent is self-love; the more self is indulged the more it demands.

154.   What makes us discontented with our condition is the absurdly exaggerated idea we have of the happiness of others.

Discretion

155.   Sometimes the best gain is to lose.

156.   Better lose the anchor than the whole ship.

—Dutch

157.   Mention not a rope in the house of one whose father was hanged.

Disturbance

158. A plant often removed cannot thrive.

Doctor—Doctors

159. No man is a good physician who has never been sick.

—Arabian

160. If the doctor cures, the sun sees it; if he kills, the earth hides it.

161. Polygamy ought to be obligatory on physicians. It would be only just to compel those who depopulate the world to repopulate it a little.

—French

Drinking

162. Drink injures a man externally, internally, and eternally.

163. Drinking a little too much is drinking a great deal too much.

—German

164. First the man takes a drink, then the drink takes a drink, then the drink takes the man.

—Japanese

Drunkenness

165. He who quarrels with a drunken man injures the absent.

E

Economy

166. There is no economy in going to bed early to save candles if the result is twins.

—Chinese

Education

167. Better untaught than ill taught.

168. Knowledge in youth is wisdom in age.

169. Learning is like rowing upstream; not to advance is to drop back.

—Chinese

170. Those who do not study are only cattle dressed up in men's clothes.

—Chinese

171. By nature all men are alike, but by education become different.

Efficiency

172. Better go than send.

—Chinese

Effort

173. Life without endeavor is like entering a jewel-mine and coming out with empty hands.

—Japanese

Enemy—Enemies

174. An open enemy is better than a false friend.

—Greek

175. There is no such thing as an insignificant enemy.

—French

176. One enemy can harm you more than a hundred friends can do you good.

—German

177. One enemy is too much for a man in a great post, and a hundred friends are too few.

Envy

178. Never envy a man unless you are willing to swap identities with him.

179. Don't just envy another's good fortune; emulate the work that helped earn it.

Epigram—Epigrams

180.   He misses what is meant by epigram
Who thinks it only frivolous flim-flam.

Equality

181. The only real equality is in the cemetery.

—German

182. If all men were on an equality, the consequence would be that all must perish; for who would till the ground? who would sow it? who would plant? who would press wine?

—Latin

Equivocation

183. Equivocation is first cousin to a lie.

Escape

184. Of all the thirty-six alternatives, running away is the best.

—Chinese

Esteem

185. Many are esteemed, only because they are not known.

—French

Exaggeration

186. Exaggeration is to paint a snake and add legs.

187. The archer who overshoots misses as well as he that falls short.

Example—Examples

188. A good example is the best sermon.

189. We reform others unconsciously when we act uprightly.

190. What can't be done by advice can often be done by example.

191. Example may be better than precept, but together they make a winning team.

192. A man profits more by the sight of an idiot than by the orations of the learned.

—Arabian

Excess—Excessiveness

193. All sunshine makes the desert.

—Arabian

194. To go beyond is as bad as to fall short.

—Chinese

Experience

195. To know the road ahead ask those coming back.

—Chinese

196. He who has been bitten by a snake is afraid of an eel.

197. Experience is a comb which nature gives to men when they are bald.

198. Experience without learning is better than learning without experience.

—American

199. A gem is not polished without rubbing, nor a man made perfect without trials.

—Chinese

Extravagance

200. He who buys what he needs not, sells what he needs.

—Japanese

Exuberance

201. In the midst of great joy do not promise to give a man anything; in the midst of great anger do not answer a man's letter.

—Chinese

F

Failure

202. Failure teaches success.

203. In great attempts it is glorious even to fail.

204. Nothing good is failure and no evil thing success.

Faith

205. He who loses money loses much. He who loses a friend loses more. But he who loses faith loses all.

Falsehood

206. Half a fact is a whole falsehood.

207. This is the punishment of a liar: he is not believed, even when he speaks the truth.

Fame

208. All fame is dangerous; good bringeth envy, bad shame.

209. Fame like a river is narrowest at its source and broadest afar off.

Familiarity

210. Caress your dog and he'll spoil your clothes.

Family

211. A child tells in the street what its father and mother say at home.

212. It is better to be the best of a low family than the worst of a noble one.

—Greek

Father—Son

213. He that does not bring up his son to some honest calling and employment, brings him up to be a thief.

Fatherhood

214. A father loves his children in hating their faults.

Fault—Faults

215. Forget others' faults by remembering your own.

216. Bad men excuse their faults; good men abandon them.

217. A fault confessed is a fault redressed; a fault once denied is twice committed.

218. Think of your own faults the first part of the night when you are awake, and the faults of others the latter part of the night when you are asleep.

—Chinese

Fault-Finding

219. He that finds fault wants to buy.

—German

220. Don't find fault with what you don't understand.

—French

Favor—Favors

221. A favor is half granted when gracefully refused.

222. The greater the favor, the greater the obligation.

Fear

223. The greater the fear the nearer the danger.

—Danish

224. Fear carries a man farther than courage—but not in the same direction.

Flattery

225. A flatterer is a secret enemy.

—Hungarian

226. A flatterer has water in one hand and fire in the other.

—German

227. Beware of one who flatters unduly; he will also censure unjustly.

—Arabian

228. He who praises me on all occasions is a fool who despises me or a knave who wishes to cheat me.

—Chinese

Flowers

229. A country where flowers are priced so as to make them a luxury has yet to learn the first principles of civilization.

—Chinese

Folly

230. A fool with money to burn soon meets his match.

231. Every man is a fool in some man's opinion.

—Spanish

232. A fool is like all other men as long as he remains silent.

—Danish

233. He who would make a fool of himself will find many to help him.

—Danish

234. He that makes himself an ass must not take it ill if men ride him.

235. A foolish man may be known by six things: Anger without cause, speech without profit, change without progress, inquiry without object, putting trust in a stranger, and mistaking foes for friends.

—Arabian

Forgetting

236.   My skirt with tears is always wet—
I have forgotten to forget.

—Japanese

Forgiveness

237. Never ask pardon before you are accused.

238. Forgiving the unrepentant is like drawing pictures on water.

—Japanese

Fraud

239. It is fraud to conceal fraud.

—Legal maxim

Freedom

240. Who accepts from another sells his freedom.

—German

Friendship

241. Friendship is love with understanding.

242. Life without a friend is death without a witness.

243. False friends are worse than open enemies.

244. When a friend asks, there is no tomorrow.

245. Who seeks a faultless friend rests friendless.

—Turkish

246. He that seeks to have many friends never has any.

—Italian

247. A courageous foe is better than a cowardly friend.

248. It's poor friendship that needs to be constantly bought.

249. Money lent to a friend must be recovered from an enemy.

—German

250. Anyone with a heart full of friendship has a hard time finding enemies.

251. He never was a friend who ceased to be so for a slight cause.

—Portuguese

252. He who puts a friend to public shame is as guilty as a murderer.

—Hebrew

253. You can hardly make a friend in a year, but you can easily offend one in an hour.

—Chinese

254. Just as tall trees are known by their shadows, so are good men known by their enemies.

—Chinese

255. An act by which we make one friend and one enemy is a losing game, because revenge is more active than gratitude.

Future, The

256. He that will not look forward must look behind.

—Gaelic

257. To worry about tomorrow is to be unhappy today.

258. One generation plants the trees . . . another gets the shade.

—Chinese

G

Gambling

259. Losing comes of winning money.

—Chinese

260. There is no better gambling than not to gamble.

—German

Genius

261. Oddities and singularities of behavior may attend genius, but they are its blemishes.

Gentleman

262. When two men quarrel, he who is first silent, is the greater gentleman.

Gift—Gifts

263. Gifts should be handed, not thrown.

−Danish

264. What is bought is cheaper than a gift.

−Portuguese

Giving

265. A shroud has no pockets.

266. No man can give what he has not.

−Legal maxim

267. A gift long expected is sold, not given.

−Italian

268. Much is expected where much is given.

269. Ask thy purse what thou shouldst spend.

−Scottish

270. He who gives when he is asked has waited too long.

271. When the hand ceases to scatter, the heart ceases to pray.

−Irish

272. If everyone gives one thread, the poor man will have a shirt.

−Russian

273. A bit of fragrance always clings to the hand that gives you roses.

−Chinese

274. They who give have all things; they who withhold have nothing.

−Hindu

275. What I gave, I have; what I spent, I had; what I kept, I lost.

276. All we can hold in our cold dead hands is what we have given away.

—Sanskrit

277. The generous man enriches himself by giving; the miser hoards himself poor.

—Dutch

278. Flowers leave a part of their fragrance in the hands that bestow them.

—Chinese

279. He who gives little gives from his heart; he who gives much gives from his wealth.

—Turkish

280. What you give for the cause of charity in health is gold; what you give in sickness is silver; what you give after death is lead.

—Jewish

281. I gave a beggar from my little store of well-earned gold. He spent the shining ore and came again, and yet again, still cold and hungry as before. I gave a thought, and through the thought of mine he found himself, the man, supreme, divine! Fed, clothed, and crowned with blessings manifold, and now he begs no more.

—Persian

Glory

282. When glory comes, loss of memory follows.

—French

283. It is a worthier thing to deserve honor than to possess it.

God

284. When the need is highest, God is nighest.

—Hebrew

285. God promises a safe landing but not a calm passage.

—Bulgarian

God—Man

286. Fear that man who fears not God.

Golden Rule

287. Do unto others as though you were others.

Good—Goodness

288. When you are good to others you are best to yourself.
—American

Gossip

289. Who gossips to you will gossip of you.
—Turkish

290. If what we see is doubtful, how can we believe what is spoken behind the back.
—Chinese

Gratitude

291. Do not cut down the tree that gives you shade.
—Arabian

292. When you drink from the stream remember the spring.
—Chinese

293. He merits no thanks who does a kindness for his own ends.

294. Gratitude is the least of virtues; ingratitude the worst of vices.

Greatness

295. A man is judged to be great because of the positive qualities he possesses; not because of the absence of faults.

Greed

296. If you chase two hares, both will escape you.

297. The ass went seeking for horns and lost his ears.

—Arabian

298. Never try to catch two frogs with one hand.

—Chinese

299. Two watermelons cannot be held under one arm.

—Turkish

300. Who seeks more than he needs hinders himself from enjoying what he has.

—Hebrew

Guilt

301. The guilty catch themselves.

302. A guilty conscience needs no accuser.

303. He confesses his guilt who evades a trial.

304. He who is guilty believes all men speak ill of him.

—Italian

Gullibility

305. If we don't stand for something, we will fall for anything.

306. It is an equal failing to trust everybody, and to trust nobody.

H

Habit—Habits

307. Bad habits indulged in become crimes.

308. Habits are cobwebs at first; cables at last.

—Chinese

309. Habits if not resisted soon become necessity.

310. Good habits result from resisting temptation.

311. A nail is driven out by another nail; habit is overcome by habit.

—Latin

Happiness

312. 'Tis not good to be happy too young.

313. Do not speak of your own happiness to one who is unhappy.

314. The secret of happiness is to count your blessings while others are adding up their troubles.

315. Taking the first step with the good thought, the second with the good word, and the third with the good deed, I enter paradise.

—Persian

Haste

316. Hasty climbers have sudden falls.

—English

317. The hasty and the tardy meet at the ferry.

—Arabian

318. Do not be in a hurry to tie what you cannot untie.

319. He who pours water hastily into a bottle spills more than goes in.

—Spanish

Hate—Hatred

320. Hatred is self-punishment.

321. As the best wine makes the sharpest vinegar, so the deepest love turns to the deadliest hatred.

Health

322. He who has health, has hope; and he who has hope, has everything.

—Arabian

Helpfulness

323. A candle loses nothing by lighting another candle.

Hero—Heroism

324. Take away ambition and vanity, and what becomes of your hero?

History

325. He that would know what shall be must consider what hath been.

Honesty

326. Honest men are easily deceived.

327. It pays to be honest, but it's slow pay.

328. Lock your door and keep your neighbor honest.

—Chinese

329. Honesty is like an icicle; if once it melts that is the end of it.

—American

330. While it pays to be honest you are often a long time collecting.

331. Honesty is a question of right and wrong, not a matter of policy.

332. He who is passionate and hasty, is generally honest; it is your cool dissembling hypocrite, of whom you should beware.

Hope

333. A misty morning does not signify a cloudy day.

Hospitality

334. A daily guest is a thief in the kitchen.

335. Who practices hospitality entertains God himself.

336. It is a sin against hospitality, to open your doors and darken your countenance.

Humility

337. Falling hurts least those who fly low.

—Chinese

338. Light-houses don't ring bells and fire cannon to call attention to their shining; they just shine on.

Humor, Sense of

339. A man without mirth is like a wagon without springs

340. A sense of humor is the pole that adds balance to our steps as we walk the tightrope of life.

Husband—Wife

341. What a husband forbids, a wife desires.

—French

342. The wife of a careless man is almost a widow.

—Hungarian

343. When a wife sins the husband is never innocent.

—Italian

344. The more a husband loves his wife the more he increases her whims.

—Chinese

345. A woman needs three husbands: one to support her, one to love her, and one to beat her.

—Bulgarian

I

Idea—Ideas

346. To possess ideas is to gather flowers; to think, is to weave them into garlands.

Idleness

347. A pound of idleness weighs twenty ounces.

Ignorance

348. An illiterate wise man is not half so dangerous as an educated fool.

349. Faults of ignorance are excusable only where the ignorance itself is so.

350. It is as great a virtue to hide ignorance as to discover knowledge.

351. The essence of knowledge is to properly apply it, not having it, to confess your ignorance.

Imitation

352. We are what we are; we gain nothing by copying others.

Impossible, The

353. By asking for the impossible we obtain the possible.

—Italian

Impudence

354. Impudence is often the result of ignorance.

Inaction

355. Doing nothing is doing evil.

356. The thought that leads to no action is not thought—it is dreaming.

357. Anyone who is satisfied to stand still should not complain when others pass him.

Incompleteness

358. Doing things by halves is worthless. It may be the other half that counts.

Inconsequence—Inconsequential

359. When small men cast big shadows, it means the sun is about to set.

Inconsistency

360. It's useless to put your best foot forward—and then drag the other.

Indecision

361. Indecision is the graveyard of good intentions.

362. While we consider when to begin, it becomes too late.

—Latin

363. When a man has not a good reason for doing a thing, he has one good reason for letting it alone.

Index

364. A book without an index is like a mind without a memory.

Infallibility

365. The man who never makes a mistake always takes orders from one who does.

Ingratitude

366. A thankless man rarely does a thankful deed.

367. Cast no dirt into the well that gives you water.

Inheritance

368. The tears of an heir are laughter under a mask.

—Latin

369. He who waits for a dead man's shoes is in danger of going barefoot.

—Danish

Injustice

370. It is easier for some people to do themselves an injustice than it is for them to do someone else a favor.

Innocence

371. A mind conscious of innocence laughs at the lies of rumor.

—Latin

Inquisitiveness

372. He who asks a question is a fool for five minutes; he who does not ask a question remains a fool forever.

—Chinese

Insight

373. In today's complex and fast-moving world, what we need even more than foresight or hindsight is insight.

Insignificance

374. Do not despise an insignificant enemy; nor a slight wound.

—German

Instability

375. He who begins many things finishes nothing.

Integrity

376. An honest man is not the worse because a dog barks at him.

—Danish

377. With lies you may go ahead in the world—but you can never go back.

—Russian

378. There can be no friendship without confidence; and no confidence, without integrity.

379. There's no limit to the height a man can attain by remaining on the level.

Intention—Intentions

380. The smallest good deed is better than the grandest good intention.

Intrinsic

381. Rotten wood cannot be carved.

—Chinese

Irritability

382. Women are more irritable than men, the reason being that men are more irritating.

J

Jealousy

383. The jealous man poisons his own banquet, and then eats it.

384. No man is a complete failure until he begins disliking men who succeed.

385. Love may exist without jealousy, although this is rare; but jealousy may exist without love, and this is common.

Jesting

386. Never risk a joke with a man who is unable to comprehend it.

Joint Effort

387. Behind an able man there are always other able men.

—Chinese

Judge—Judges

388. An upright judge has more regard for justice than for men.

Judging

389. He who is judge between two friends loses one of them.
—French

390. He who will have no judge but himself condemns himself.

Judgment

391. Good judgment comes from experience, which comes from poor judgment.

Justice

392. Rigid justice is rank injustice.

393. Don't hang a man and then try him afterward.

394. When one divides, the other should have the right of first choice.
—Legal maxim

395. Little thieves are hanged by the neck and great thieves by the purse.

396. Justice is better when it prevents rather than punishes with severity.
—Legal maxim

397. He who allows himself to be a worm must not complain if he is trodden upon.

398. Where the law is most strictly administered, it sometimes causes the greatest wrong.
—Legal maxim

399. When a jury permits a guilty man to escape, it augments the danger of the innocent.

K

Keenness

400. It takes a rough stone to sharpen the edge.

Kindness

401. Better do a kindness near home than go far to burn incense.
—Chinese

402. Hatred and anger are powerless when met with kindness.

403. He merits no thanks who does a kindness from selfish motives.

Kiss—Kisses—Kissing

404. Don't kiss a homely maid—she'll brag of it.

Knowledge

405. Who knows most, knows least.
—Italian

406. He who increases knowledge, increases sorrow.

407. The pope and a peasant know more between them than the pope alone.
—Italian

408. He who knows not, and knows not that he
knows not, is a fool. Shun him.
He who knows not, and knows that he knows not
is simple. Teach him.

He who knows, and knows not that he knows,
  is asleep. Waken him.
He who knows, and knows that he knows is
  wise. Follow him.

—Arabian

L

Labor

409. Those who labor with their minds, rule; those who labor with their bodies, are ruled.

Landlord—Tenant

410. A tenant is not entitled to regard his house as his castle

Laughter

411. He who laughs—lasts.

—Norwegian

Law—Laws

412. A bad agreement is better than a good lawsuit.

—Italian

413. A good judge conceives quickly, judges slowly.

414. No man can make another a debtor against his will.

—Legal maxim

415. A good law unexecuted is like an unperformed promise.

Law Enforcement

416. Better no law than law not enforced.

—Danish

Lawyer—Client

417. He who is his own lawyer has a fool for a client.

418. The robes of lawyers are lined with the obstinacy of clients.

Leadership

419. One bad general is better than two good ones.

—French

420. Don't waste good iron for nails . . . good men for soldiers.

—Chinese

421. A born leader sees which way the crowd is going and steps in ahead.

422. When a large vessel has opened a way it is easy for a small one to follow.

—Chinese

423. Every leader has to look back once in a while to make sure he has followers.

424. Civilization is always in danger when those who have never learned to obey are given the right to command.

Learning

425. He who adds not to his learning diminishes it.

Legacy—Legacies

426. A man who teaches his children industry provides them with a fortune.

Legislation

427. The more laws the less justice.

—German

428. Good laws make it easier to do right and harder to do wrong.

429. We should never do by law what can be accomplished by morality.

Lending

430. He who lends to the poor gives to the Lord, who will repay him with interest.

Lie—Lies

431. Better a lie that soothes than a truth that hurts.

—Czech

Life

432. I wept when I was born and every day explains why.

—Spanish

433. He who saves one life is considered as if he had preserved the whole world.

—The Talmud

Literature

434. Literature is a candle lighted in the mind and left alight.

Litigation

435. He who has the worst cause makes the most noise.

Little Things

436. Lights of a thousand stars do not make one moon.

437. He that will not stoop for a pin will never be worth a pound.

—English

438. Do little things now; so shall big things come to thee by and by asking to be done.

—Persian

Loquacity

439. Loquacity and lying are cousins.

—German

440. To talk much and arrive nowhere is the same as climbing a tree to catch a fish.

—Chinese

Loss—Losses

441. Fortune lost, nothing lost; courage lost, much lost; honor lost, more lost; soul lost, all lost.

Love

442. They love too much that die for love.

443. One loves more the first time, better the second.

444. To love is to admire with the heart; to admire is to love with the mind.

Luck

445. Too much luck is bad luck.

—German

446. Luck never gives; it only lends.

—Swedish

447. In bad luck hold out; in good luck, hold in.

—German

448. Good and bad luck are synonyms, in the great majority of instances, for good and bad judgment.

Luxury

449. Living in the lap of luxury isn't bad, except that you never know when luxury is going to stand up.

M

Man—Men

450. Gold is tested by fire, man by gold.

—Chinese

Man—Woman

451. A woman without a man is like a garden without a fence.

—German

Marriage

452. He who marries for wealth sells his own liberty.

453. Don't marry for money; you can borrow it cheaper.

—Scotch

454. A poor man who takes a rich wife has a ruler, not a wife.

—Greek

455. A deaf husband and a blind wife are always a happy couple.

—French

456. He who marries *might* be sorry. He who does not *will* be sorry.

—Czechoslovakian

457. Marriage may be an institution but it is not a reform school.

458. One should choose a wife with the ears, rather than with the eyes.

—French

459. To marry a woman for her beauty is like buying a house for its paint.

460. When a man makes a mistake in his first marriage the victim is his second wife.

Married Life

461. The best way to keep a husband is in doubt.

462. Not all wives are suspicious—some are certain.

463. When a man sees eye to eye with his wife, it means that his vision has been corrected.

464. When a wife insists on wearing the pants, some other woman wears the fur coat.

Maxim—Maxims

465. All the good maxims have been written. It only remains to put them into practice.

Meanness

466. Even the mean man has his value. You can learn from him how not to live.

Mechanization

467. The greatest danger in modern technology isn't that machines will begin to think like men, but that men will begin to think like machines.

Meddling

468. Never burn your fingers to snuff another man's candle.

Melancholy—Melancholia

469. It is the melancholy face that gets stung by the bee.

Memory—Memories

470. Bad memory has its root in bad attention.

471. Pleasant memories must be arranged for in advance.

472. Memory was given to mortals so that they might have roses in December.

473. A good memory is one that can remember the day's blessings and forget the day's troubles.

Mercy

474. Justice tempered with too much mercy becomes injustice.

475. In case of doubt it is best to lean to the side of mercy. (*In dubiis benigniora sunt semper praeferenda.*)
—Legal maxim

Merit

476. A horse of good breed is not dishonored by his saddle.
—Arabic

477. A great name without merit is like an epitaph on a coffin.

Military

478. The common soldier's blood makes the general great.
—Italian

479. A good general not only sees the way to victory; he also knows when victory is impossible.

Mind, The

480. A wise man changes his mind, a fool never.

—Spanish

481. To change one's mind is rather a sign of prudence than ignorance.

—Spanish

482. Great minds discuss ideas, mediocre minds discuss events, small minds discuss personalities.

Miserliness

483. Fools live poor to die rich.

Misfortune

484. Misfortunes test friends, and detect enemies.

485. Misfortune can take away nothing but what good fortune gave us.

486. Misfortunes are, in morals, what bitters are in medicine: each is at first disagreeable; but as the bitters act as corroborants to the stomach, so adversity chastens and ameliorates the disposition.

—French

Mistake—Mistakes

487. He is always right who suspects that he makes mistakes.

—Spanish

488. It is disgraceful to stumble against the same stone twice.

—Greek

489. A mistake at least proves somebody stopped talking long enough to do something.

490. The man who takes time to explain his mistakes has little time left for anything else.

491. The only complete mistake is the mistake from which we learn nothing.

492. It is all right to forget your mistakes, if you remember their lessons.

493. The mistakes of the learned man are like a shipwreck which wrecks many others with it.

—Arabian

494. In order to profit from your mistakes, you have to go out and make some.

495. The man who never makes mistakes loses a great many chances to learn something.

496. If you didn't make mistakes you might live and die without ever hearing your name mentioned.

497. Mistakes are a great educator when one is honest enough to admit them and willing to learn from them.

498. About all the average person learns from his mistakes is how to be an expert in making excuses.

Misunderstanding

499. A truth that one does not understand becomes an error.

500. Be not disturbed at being misunderstood; be disturbed at not understanding.

—Chinese

501. There is no worse lie than a truth misunderstood by those who hear it.

Moderation

502. He will always be a slave who does not know how to live upon a little.

503. Moderation in temper is a virtue, but moderation in principle is always a vice.

Modern Age

504. They love the old who do not know the new.

—German

505. One of the weaknesses of our age is our apparent inability to distinguish our need from our greed.

Modesty

506. Great men never feel great. Small men never feel small.

507. He who takes his rank lightly raises his own dignity.

—Hebrew

508. One coin in the money-box makes more noise than when it is full.

—Arabian

Money

509. When money speaks, the truth is silent.

510. Money separates more friends than it unites.

511. Eloquence avails nothing against the voice of gold.

—Latin

512. What good is money to burn after the fire has gone out.

513. The hardest thing about making money last is making it first.

514. A fool may make money but it requires a wise man to spend it.

515. The only thing that many people understand about money matters is that it does.

516. To get money is difficult, to keep it more difficult, but to spend it wisely most difficult of all.

517. The person who doesn't know where his next dollar is coming from usually doesn't know where his last dollar went.

Monument

518. No monuments are erected for the righteous; their deeds perpetuate their memory.

Mother—Child

519. No gift to your mother can ever equal her gift to you—life.

Motherhood

520. The death of a mother is the first sorrow wept without her.

521. The remembrance of a beloved mother becomes a shadow to all our actions; it precedes or follows them.

Mother-In-Law

522. Happy is she who marries the son of a dead mother.
—Scottish

523. Men speak of their in-laws as if their wives didn't have any.

524. The mother-in-law frequently forgets that she was a daughter-in-law.

Mourning

525. He mourns the dead who lives as they desire.

526. The childless couple sleep in weed-covered graves.

N

Narrow-Mindedness

527. A narrow mind and a wide mouth usually go together.

Nature

528. There are in nature no rewards or punishments just consequences.

529. To pay homage to beauty is to admire Nature; to admire Nature is to worship God.

Necessity

530. That which necessity compels she excuses.
—Legal maxim

531. Necessity changes many a course but never a goal.

532. Necessity makes laws, but does not obey them.

Neighbor—Neighbors

533. No one is rich enough to do without a neighbor.
—Danish

534. Don't expect your neighbor to be better than your neighbor's neighbor.

535. The fence that makes good neighbors needs a gate to make good friends.

536. Be happy with your neighbor's prosperity because it contributes to your own.

O

Obedience

537. When you obey your superior you instruct your inferior.

538. Every great person has first learned how to obey, whom to obey, and when to obey.

Objective—Objectives

539. Obstacles always show up when you take your eyes off the goal.

Obstacle—Obstacles

540. The greater the obstacle the more glory in overcoming it.

541. An obstacle is often an unrecognized opportunity.

542. Whatever impedes a man but doesn't stop him, aids his progress.

Obstinacy

543. Fools and obstinate men make rich lawyers.

—Spanish

Obvious, The

544. The obscure we see eventually. The completely apparent takes longer.

Offensiveness

545. Keep on your *own* toes if you expect to make progress.

Old Age

546. One cannot help being old—but one can resist being aged.

547. You are old only if you'd rather win an argument than be right.

548. Many people use their youth to make their old age miserable.

549. More people would live to a ripe old age if they weren't too busy providing for it.

550. It's only natural for older people to be quiet. They have a lot more to be quiet about.

551. Old age may seem a long way off. But on the day it doesn't, it will be too late to do anything about it.

552. When you see an old man amiable, mild, equable, content, and good-humored, be sure that in his youth he has been just, generous, and forbearing. In his end he does not lament the past, nor dread the future; he is like the evening of a fine day.

—Arabic

Opinion—Opinions

553. The foolish and dead alone never change their opinion.

554. Risk little on the opinion of a man who has nothing to lose.

Opportunity—Opportunities

555. If God shuts one door, He opens another.

—Irish

556. They wrong opportunity who say she knocks but once.

557. Opportunities always look bigger going than coming.

558. The doors of opportunity are marked "Push" and "Pull."

559. When you are an anvil be patient; when a hammer, strike.

—Arabian

560. He fasted for a whole year and then broke his fast with an onion.

—Arabian

561. To recognize opportunity is the difference between success and failure.

562. The trouble with opportunity is that it always comes disguised as hard work.

563. If you want to launch big ships, you have to go where the water is deep.

564. An ostrich with its head in the sand is just as blind to opportunity as to disaster.

565. Opportunity is often missed because we are broadcasting when we should be tuning in.

566. Even when opportunity knocks a man still has to get up off his seat and open the door.

567. Better late than never is poor consolation for the man who has lost the opportunity of a lifetime.

568. If a man can afford to sit down and wait for a golden opportunity to come along he doesn't need it.

569. Opportunity has hair in front, behind she is bald; if you seize her by the forelock, you may hold her, but, if suffered to escape, not Jupiter himself can catch her again.

—Latin

Opposition

570. Taking the line of least resistance still makes both men and rivers crooked.

571. It takes a strong man to swim against the current; any dead fish will float with it.

572. It is usually easy to tell whether a proposition is right by observing the gang who thinks it is wrong.

Optimism

573. Keep your face to the sunshine and you cannot see the shadow.

574. Don't be sorry if the bottle is half empty. Be glad that it is half full.

575. A cloud cannot cast a shadow unless the sun is shining beyond it.

576. When fate knocks you flat on your back, remember she leaves you looking up.

Optimist—Pessimist

577. A pessimist finds difficulty in every opportunity; an optimist finds opportunity in every difficulty.

Oratory

578. Trying to settle a problem with oratory is like attempting to unsnarl a traffic jam by blowing horns.

Originality

579. To select well among old things is almost equal to inventing new ones.

580. If you want to be original, be yourself. God never made two people exactly alike.

581. He will never worship well the image on the altar who knew it when it was a trunk of wood in the garden.

—Spanish

Overeating

582. Eat, drink and be merry. And tomorrow you'll wish you were dead.

583. Many doctors pay their grocery bill with the money of folks who have eaten too much.

Overweight

584. Square meals make round people.

585. Seconds count—especially when dieting.

586. Some women would be more spic if they had less span.

587. The best way to lose weight is to eat all you want of everything you don't like.

P

Pain

588. An hour of pain is as long as a day of pleasure.

Parent—Child

589. Among things so simple a child can operate are parents.

590. To understand your parents' love bear your own children.
—Chinese

591. To some baffled parents youth is stranger than fiction.

592. Give your children too much freedom and you lose your own.
—Russian

593. The ability to say "no" is perhaps the greatest gift a parent has.

594. Who does not beat his own child will later beat his own breast.
—Persian

595. 'Tis better to have loved and lost than to do homework with three children.

596. Don't wait to make your son a great man—make him a great boy.

597. When parents don't mind that their children don't mind, the children don't.

598. If your children look up to you, you've made a success of life's biggest job.

599. There is only one beautiful child in the world and every mother has it.

600. A girl may be easier to raise than a boy, but she is also harder to get rid of.

601. A wise parent is one who knows which side his brood should be battered on.

602. The easiest way to teach children the value of money is to borrow some from them.

603. Discipline doesn't break a child's spirit half as often as the lack of it breaks a parent's heart.

604. Parents who are afraid to put their foot down usually have children who step on their toes.

—Chinese

605. Parents wonder why the streams are bitter when they themselves have poisoned the fountain.

606. Children who avoid the mistakes their parents made often make the mistakes their parents avoided.

607. One of the first things one notices in a backward country is that children are still obeying their parents.

608. One reason there are so many juvenile delinquents today is that their dads didn't burn their britches behind them.

609. It is more important to know where your children are tonight than where your ancestors were when the *Mayflower* sailed.

610. If our boys and girls are not so good as they were when you were a child their age, it may be that they had a much better mother and dad than your child has.

Parenthood

611. Cows forget that they were calves.

612. Good fathers make good sons.

613. Very frequently rich parents make poor parents.

614. He is unworthy of life who gives no life to another.
—Latin

615. Parents should work together as efficiently as two book ends.

616. Some parents really bring their children up; others let them down.

617. Too many parents are not on spanking terms with their children.

618. The accent may be on youth, but the stress is still on parents.

619. Parents used to strike children to discipline them. Now it is usually in self-defense.

620. Out of the mouths of babes come words we shouldn't have said in the first place.

621. Children begin by loving their parents. As they grow older, they judge them. Sometimes they forgive them.

622. Parents who are always giving their children nothing but the best usually wind up with nothing but the worst.

623. When parents spoil their children, it is less to please them than to please themselves. It is the egotism of parental love.

Parting

624. To part is to die a little.

Partnership

625. He who takes a partner takes a master.

—French

626. The partner of my partner is not my partner.

—Legal maxim

Passions

627. Where passion is high, there reason is low.

628. He that overcomes his passions, overcomes his greatest enemies.

Past, The

629. No man can call again yesterday.

630. The mill cannot grind with the water that is past.

631. The past is valuable as a guidepost, but dangerous if used as a hitching post.

632. Sometimes when a man recalls the good old days, he's really thinking of his bad young days.

Past—Present—Future

633. Look upon the present as the past of your future.

634. The foundations for a better tomorrow must be laid today.

635. Good cheer is something more than faith in the future, it is gratitude for the past and joy in the present.

636. You can't change the past, but you can ruin the present by worrying about the future.

637. To prepare for the future, examine the present. To understand the present, study the past.

638. Every man's life lies within the present; for the past is spent and done with, and the future is uncertain.

639. Historians tell us about the past and economists tell us about the future. Thus only the present is confusing.

640. It is not the experience of today that drives men mad; it is remorse or bitterness for something which happened yesterday and the dread of what tomorrow may bring.

Patience

641. Patience is bitter, but its fruit is sweet.

—French

642. The anvil lasts longer than the hammer.

643. Patience under old injuries invites new ones.

644. One minute of patience, ten years of peace.

—Greek

645. Patience and the mulberry leaf become a silk robe.

—Chinese

646. A man is as big as the things that annoy him.

647. An ounce of patience is worth a pound of brains.

—Dutch

648. Patience does not mean indifference; it is the art of hoping.

649. What cannot be removed, becomes lighter through patience.

—Latin

650. The secret of patience is doing something else in the meanwhile.

651. Patience is good only when it is the shortest way to a good end; otherwise, impatience is better.

652. Sometimes we take credit for being patient when we are simply putting off doing something unpleasant.

653. Only those who have the patience to do simple things perfectly ever acquire the skill to do difficult things easily.

Patriotism

654. A good citizen owes his life to his country.

—Russian

655. Patriotism is the last refuge of a scoundrel.

—Dr. Samuel Johnson

656. The proper means of increasing the love we bear to our native country is to reside some time in a foreign one.

Peace

657. To be enduring, a peace must be endurable.

658. It also takes two to make up after a quarrel.

659. The best way to end a war is not to begin it.

660. A deceitful peace is more hurtful than open war.

661. What the world needs is the peace that surpasses all misunderstandings.

662. No doubt peace hath its victories, but what the world needs is a victory that hath its peace.

663. One does not like hot, the other does not like cold; make it tepid to make an agreement.

—Malagasy

664. If there is righteousness in the heart there will be beauty in the character. If there be beauty in the character, there will be harmony in the home. If there is harmony in the home, there will be order in the nation. When there is order in the nation, there will be peace in the world.

—Chinese

People

665. Too many of us are like wheelbarrows—useful only when pushed and too easily upset.

Perfection

666. A gem is not polished without rubbing, nor a man made perfect without trials.

Performance

667. Pressure is on us by the nature of the job. Performance releases pressure.

668. You are doing your best only when you are trying to improve what you are doing.

669. The feeling that you've done a job well is rewarding; the feeling that you've done it perfectly is fatal.

Persecution

670. To persecute the unfortunate is like throwing stones on one fallen into a well.

—Chinese

Perseverance

671. Little and often make much.

672. It is often the last key on the ring which opens the door.

673. Look for a thing until you find it and you'll not lose your labor.

—Chinese

674. The hard part of making good is that you have to do it every day.

675. If you get up one time more than you fall you will make it through.

676. Stopping at third base adds no more to the score than striking out.

677. Keep trying. It's only from the valley that the mountain seems high.

678. The great question is not whether you have failed, but whether you are content with failure.

679. To get through the hardest journey we need take only one step at a time, but we must keep on stepping.

680. If you want a crop for one year, grow millet. If you want a crop for ten years, grow a tree. If you want a crop for one hundred years, grow men.

—Chinese

Personality

681. Personality has the power to open many doors, but character must keep them open.

Pettiness

682. Those who apply themselves too closely to little things become incapable of great things.

Philanthropy

683. What is done for another is done for oneself.

—Latin

Pity

684. He that pities another remembers himself.

685. He who would have others pity him must pity others.

—Yiddish

Plan—Plans—Planning

686. Wishing consumes as much energy as planning.

Pleasure—Pleasures

687. Pleasures are transient, honors are immortal.

—Greek

Point of View

688. We are inclined to see things not as they are, but as we are.

689. If anyone is not willing to accept your point of view, try to see his point of view.

—Lebanese

690. We're all salesmen of our wares and things look a lot different from the other side of the counter.

Politeness

691. Politeness wins the confidence of princes.

—Chinese

692. If you bow at all, bow low.

—Chinese

693. Politeness is what warmth is to wax.

—German

694. A civil denial is better than a rude grant.

695. Politeness is the most acceptable hypocrisy.

696. Anyone can be polite to a king. It takes a gentleman to be polite to a beggar.

697. A polite man is one who listens with interest to things he knows all about when they are told to him by a person who knows nothing about them.

Politician—Politicians

698. Some politicians repair their fences by hedging.

699. A politician is known by the promises he keeps.

700. The politician who can be bought sooner or later gives himself away.

701. A statesman is an ex-politician who has mastered the art of holding his tongue.

702. A statesman tries to arouse the nation whereas a politician lulls it to sleep.

703. We all work for the government but the politician is wise. He gets paid for it.

Politics

704. If you can't lick 'em, join 'em.

—American

705. Politics makes berths for strange fellows.

706. Only fools are glad when governments change.

—Rumanian

707. In politics a man must learn to rise above principle.

—American

708. Some go into politics not to do good, but to do well.

709. The cheaper the politician, the more he costs his country.

710. All political parties die at last by swallowing their own lies.

711. To err is human, to blame it on the other party is politics.

712. A political landslide buries almost everything except the hatchet.

713. We need a law that will permit a voter to sue a candidate for breach of promise.

714. Many a man goes into politics with a fine future and comes out with a terrible past.

715. Political difference is good for democracy. It's political indifference that's harmful.

716. Politics is inherently clean. It becomes dirty only when it is badly administered by supposedly good citizens.

717. Any businessman who says he is not interested in politics is like a drowning man who insists he is not interested in water.

718. If you lie to people to get their money, that's fraud. If you lie to them to get their vote, that's politics.

719. To live with our enemies as if they may some time become our friends, and to live with our friends as if they may some time become our enemies, is not a moral but a political maxim.

Pomposity

720. There's nothing quite as empty as a stuffed shirt.

Popularity

721. God will not love thee less, because men love thee more.

Position

722. At a round table there's no dispute.

Possession—Possessions

723. You cannot lose what you never had.

724. Everything goes to him who wants nothing.

—French

725. All strive to give to him who already has.

726. You can never consider that as you own which can be changed.

—Latin

Poverty

727. Poverty is death in another form.

—Latin

728. To have nothing is not poverty.

—Latin

729. Poverty is not a shame, but the being ashamed of it is.

730. Painless poverty is better than embittered wealth.

—Greek

731. He who is ashamed of his poverty would be equally proud of his wealth.

732. A man can stand his own poverty better than he can the other fellow's prosperity.

733. The poor are rightfully the property of the rich, because the rich made them.

734. If you can keep yourself with poverty you have no need of riches.

—Danish

735. The poorest man in the world is the one who is always wanting more than he has.

736. Why do people try so hard to conceal poverty at the time they are experiencing it and then brag about it so in their memoirs?

Power

737. Power buries those who wield it.

738. All power is a compound of time and patience.

739. The less power a man has, the more he likes to use it.

740. Power acquired by guilt was never used for a good purpose.
—Latin

Praise

741. Fool's praise is censure.

742. Faint praise is disparagement.

743. He who praises everybody praises nobody.

744. Praise a fool and you may make him useful.

745. In doing what we ought we deserve no praise.
—Latin

746. Forbear to mention what thou canst not praise.

747. Praise makes good men better and bad men worse.

748. The highest praise for a man is to give him responsibility.

749. Never praise a woman for possessing masculine traits.

750. Judicious praise is to children what the sun is to flowers.

751. Modesty is the only sure bait when you angle for praise.

752. An honest man is hurt by praise unjustly bestowed.
—French

753. We praise willingly in others those merits which we fancy we ourselves possess.

754. It is the greatest possible praise to be praised by a man who is himself deserving of praise.
—Latin

755. It is better to say something good about a bad man, than something bad about a good man.

756. From praise, as from a shadow, a man is neither bigger nor smaller.
—Danish

757. Praise is like a shadow. It follows him who flees from it, but flees from him who follows it.

758. Be moderate in praising a man when he is present, but give him full credit when he is absent.

759. The trouble with most of us is that we would rather be ruined by praise than saved by criticism.

760. If our aim is to praise, we should forget to criticize; if our aim is to criticize, we should remember to praise.

761. Do not praise thy friend too much, for in speaking of his good qualities thou wilt touch upon his bad ones.

Prayer

762. Pray devoutly, but hammer stoutly.

763. Prayers go up and blessings come down.
—Yiddish

764. The family that prays together stays together.

765. If you are too busy to pray, you are too busy.

766. Don't pray for lighter burdens, but for stronger backs.

767. There is a vast difference between saying prayers and—praying.

768. Many prayers remain unanswered, pending endorsement of our deeds.

769. Prayer doesn't change things. It changes people, and they change things.

770. He who fails to pray does not cheat God, he cheats himself.

771. All prayers are answered if we are willing to admit that sometimes the answer is "no."

Preacher—Preachers—Preaching

772. There are many preachers who don't hear themselves.

773. Too many sermons are hung on texts like hats on a hat-tree.

774. The best preacher is the heart; the best teacher is time; the best book is the world; the best friend is God.

775. The average man's idea of a good sermon is one that goes over his head—and hits one of his neighbors.

Precaution

776. A danger foreseen is half avoided.

777. The stitch is lost unless the thread be knotted.

—Italian

778. When your neighbor's house is on fire, carry water to your own.

—Italian

Precocity

779. He dies before he is old who is wise before his day.

—Latin

Prejudice

780. Prejudice is the reason of fools.

781. Men are blind in their own cause.

—American

782. No prejudice has even been able to prove its case in the court of reason.

Premature—Prematurity

783. Never ask pardon before you are accused.

784. Don't celebrate a holiday before it arrives.

785. Do not rejoice over what has not yet happened.

—Egyptian

786. He who has not yet reached the opposite shore should not make fun of him who is drowning.

—Guinea

Preoccupation

787. Prejudice cannot see the things that are because it is always looking for things that aren't.

Preparation

788. A barber always lathers his customer before he shaves him.

Preparedness

789. Hope for the best, but be ever ready for the worst.

790. When you're thirsty it's too late to think about digging a well.

—Japanese

Presence

791. A person is present wherever his presence is felt.

Pretense

792. A stuffed shirt is usually all front.

793. Intentions which die are pretensions which lie.

Prevention

794. Hindsight explains the injury that foresight would have prevented.

795. It is better to keep a friend from falling than to help him up.

Pride

796. The nobler the blood the less the pride.

797. He that is too proud to ask is too good to receive.

798. There is no pride like that of a beggar grown rich.

—French

799. Temper gets people into trouble. Pride keeps them there.

800. A man may have a just esteem of himself without being proud.

801. No one with a good catch of fish goes home by way of the back alley.

Problem—Problems

802. The important thing about a problem is not its solution, but the strength we gain in finding the solution.

Procrastination

803. One of these days is none of these days.

804. Many fine things can be done in a day if you don't always make that day tomorrow.

Professional Fees

805. A physician whose services are obtained gratis is worth nothing.

Profit—Profits

806. Small profits and often, are better than large profits and seldom.

—German

Profundity

807. When the river is deepest it makes least noise.

Progress

808. A house pulled down is half rebuilt.

809. Progress begins with getting a clear view of the obstacles..

Prominence

810. If you want a place in the sun, you've got to expect a few blisters.

Promise—Promises

811. A promise is a debt.

812. A promise against law or duty is void in its own nature.

813. We make large promises to avoid making small presents.

814. When a man repeats a promise again and again he means to fail you.

815. Promises are like the full moon, if they are not kept at once they diminish day by day.

—German

Promotion

816. People who get down to brass tacks usually rise rapidly.

Property

817. He who feeds the hen ought to have the egg.

—Danish

Prosperity

818. In prosperity we need moderation; in adversity, patience.

Proverb—Proverbs

819. A proverb never lies, it is only its meaning which deceives.

—German

820. The proverb answers where the sermon fails as a well-charged pistol will do more execution than a whole barrel of gunpowder idly exploded in the air.

821. The wisdom of nations lies in their proverbs, which are brief and pithy. Collect and learn them; they are notable measures and directions for human life; you have much in little; they save time in speaking; and upon occasion may be the fullest and safest answers.

Prudence

822. I'd rather have them say "There he goes" than "Here he lies."

—American

Prudery

823. Prudery is the hypocrisy of modesty.

Public Office

824. When an official has no opposition, the people will soon have no choice.

Public Rights

825. A public right cannot be changed by private agreement.

—Legal maxim

Public Speaking

826. Poets are born but orators are made.

827. If oratory is a lost art, let's leave it that way.

828. Speaking without thinking is shooting without taking aim.

Punctuality

829. Happy is the man who is always early—if he can stand the loneliness.

830. The trouble with being punctual is that there's nobody there to appreciate it.

Punishment

831. Who punishes one threatens a hundred.

—French

832. Man punishes the action, but God the intention.

833. It is a cruelty to the innocent not to punish the guilty.

Purpose

834. He will go far, who knows from the first whither he is going.

Q

Quality

835. There never was a good knife made of bad steel.

836. Buying a cheap article to save money is like stopping the clock to save time.

837. The bitterness of poor quality lingers long after the sweetness of cheap price is forgotten.

Quarrel—Quarrels

838. Two cannot fall out if one does not choose.

—Spanish

839. A chip on the shoulder indicates there is wood higher up.

840. Quarrels do not last long if the wrong is only on one side.

—French

841. 'Tis better keeping off a quarrel, than to make it up afterwards.

842. A quarrel is like buttermilk, once it's out of the churn, the more you shake it, the more sour it grows.

—Irish

Quest

843. The fun is in the search, not the finding. The thrill is in the chase, not the quarry.

844. To be forever reaching out, to remain unsatisfied, is the key to spiritual progress.

Question—Answer

845. Never answer a question until it is asked.

846. Avoid a questioner, for he is also a tattler.

847. Ask me no questions and I'll tell you no lies.

848. The man who is afraid of asking is ashamed of learning.

—Danish

849. When you know all the answers, you haven't asked all the questions.

850. A fool may ask more questions in an hour than a wise man can answer in seven years.

—English

Quid Pro Quo

851. When somebody gets something for nothing, somebody else usually gets nothing for something.

Quit—Quitter—Quitting

852. To quit while losing is to lose while quitting.

Quotation—Quotations

853. A fine quotation is a diamond on the finger of a man of wit, and a pebble in the hand of a fool.

—French

R

Readiness

854. The day I did not sweep the house there came to it one I did not expect.

Reading

855. Beware of the man of one book.

—Latin

856. Few are better than the books they read.

857. Life is too short for reading inferior books.

858. The art of reading is to skip judiciously.

859. There is no worse robber than a bad book.

·Italian

860. The man who doesn't read good books has no advantage over the man who can't read them.

Reason

861. Nothing can be lasting when reason does not rule.

—Latin

Reciprocity

862. One nail drives out another.

—German

863. If a person shave you with a razor, do not shave him with broken glass.

—Surinam

864. If you do not strike back at him who hits you, there is no way for him to find out whether you also have hands.

—Russian

Reconciliation

865. Even in a quarrel, leave room for reconciliation.

—Russian

Recreation

866. Time you enjoy wasting is not wasted time.

Reform—Reforms

867. To innovate is not to reform.

868. Every generation needs regeneration.

869. Every reform movement has a lunatic fringe.

870. Every reform needs examples more than advocates.

871. In our haste to deal with the things which are wrong, let us not upset the things which are right.

Refusal

872. Man counts what he has refused, not what he has given.

—Kikuyu (Kenya Colony)

Regret

873. Regret is insight that comes a day too late.

874. No man is rich enough to buy back his past.

875. The follies a man regrets most are the ones he didn't commit when he could.

Relative—Relatives

876. The one-eyed person is a beauty in the country of the blind.
—Arabian

877. Relatives are the worst friends, said the fox as the dogs took after him.

—Danish

Religion

878. Religion is either applied or denied.

879. Religion is a journey, not a destination.

880. Religions are many, but Religion is one.

881. No man's religion ever survives his morals.
—English

882. Without religion, educated men become devils.

883. To you your religion; and to me my religion.
—Islam

884. Monday religion is better than Sunday profession.

885. A man devoid of religion is like a horse without a bridle.
—Latin

886. The religion of one age is the poetry of the next.

887. To be furious in religion is to be irreligiously religious.

888. Religion often gets credit for curing rascals when old age is the real medicine.

889. Religion is meant to be bread for daily use, not cake for special occasions.

890. In religion, as in friendship, they who profess most are the least sincere.

891. One of the aims of religion is to encourage us to live the way we say we believe.

892. Human things must be known to be loved; but Divine things must be loved to be known.

Religion—Science

893. It is better to inspire the heart with a noble sentiment than to teach the mind a truth of science.

Repentance

894. Amendment is repentance.

895. Not to repent of a fault is to justify it.

896. Repentance is good, but innocence better.

897. The sinning is the best part of repentance.

—Arabian

898. Repentance for silence is better than repentance for speaking.

—Moorish

Repercussion

899. Don't teach archery lest you become the target.

Reproach

900. The sting of a reproach is the truth of it.

—English

Reputation

901. Every tub smells of the wine it holds.

902. No man was written out of reputation but by himself.

903. Don't consider your reputation and you may do anything you like.

—Chinese

904. The reputation of a man is like his shadow: it sometimes follows and sometimes precedes him, it is sometimes longer and sometimes shorter than his natural size.

—French

Responsibility

905. Responsibility develops some men and ruins others.

906. Some men grow under responsibility, others only swell.

907. That which is everybody's business is nobody's business.

908. He who lets the goat be laid on his shoulders is soon after forced to carry the cow.

—Italian

Retribution

909. As you make your bed, so shall you lie in it.

910. He who pelts every barking dog must pick up many stones.

911. He that plants thorns must never expect to gather roses.
—Arabian

Revenge

912. Living well is the best revenge.

913. Revenge is a confession of pain.
—Latin

914. To forget a wrong is the best revenge.

915. He meditates revenge who least complains.

916. Neglect will sooner kill an injury than revenge.

917. Revenge does not long remain unrevenged.
—German

918. If you want to be revenged, hold your tongue.
—Spanish

919. To take revenge is often to sacrifice oneself.
—Kongo (Belgian Congo)

920. The longest odds in the world are those against getting even.

921. Time spent in getting even would be better spent in getting ahead.

922. A man need never revenge himself, the body of his enemy will be brought to his own door.
—Chinese

Revolution—Revolutions

923. Revolutions never go backwards.

924. Every revolution was first a thought in one man's mind.

Reward

925. Service without reward is punishment.

926. The reward of a thing rightly done is to have done it.
—Latin

927. The highest reward for a man's toil is not what he gets for it but rather what he becomes by it.

Rich—Riches

928. God help the rich, the poor can beg.

929. It is better to live rich than to die rich.

930. He is not fit for riches who is afraid to use them.

931. Riches are gotten with pain, kept with care, and lost with grief.

Ridicule

932. Ridicule is the test of truth.

933. There are few who would not rather be hated than laughed at.

Right

934. There is no right way to do a wrong thing.

Righteousness

935. A good way to widen out the narrow path would be for more people to walk on it.

Rivalry

936. A person is truly great when he is not envious of his rival's success.

Romance

937. Old flames seem to burn forever.

938. Girls who play with fire seldom strike a match.

939. Some girls play hard to get until they become hard to take.

940. Sometimes the law of gravity doesn't work; for instance, it's easier to pick up a girl than it is to drop her.

Rudeness

941. Rudeness is a weak man's imitation of strength.

942. Three of the rudest people in the world are: a young fellow making fun of an old man, a strong person jeering at an invalid, a wise man mocking a fool.

Rumor

943. A mind conscious of innocence laughs at the lies of rumor.

Rust

944. Better to wear out than to rust out.

945. The brightest blades grow dim with rust.

S

Sacrifice

946. Drown not thyself to save a drowning man.

947. Not even for the highest principles has anyone the right to sacrifice others than himself.

Safety

948. The way to be safe is never to feel secure.

949. He who goes the lowest builds the safest.

950. The only safety for the conquered is to expect no safety.

Sailing

951. Being in a ship is like being in a jail, with the chance of being drowned.

Salesmanship

952. Selling is easy if you work hard enough at it.

953. Cash can buy, but it takes enthusiasm to sell.

954. The object of a salesman is not to make sales, but to make customers.

955. Good salesmanship consists in selling goods that won't come back to customers who will.

956. It takes less effort to keep an old customer satisfied than to get a new customer interested.

Salvation

957. The fearless man is his own salvation.

958. The knowledge of sin is the beginning of salvation.

—Latin

Satiety

959. A woman is a well-served table that one sees with different eyes before and after the meal.

—French

Saving

960. What you save is, later, like something found.

—Yiddish

Scandal

961. Scandal and failure make news—only success makes history.

962. A lot of molehills become mountains when someone adds a little dirt.

963. That which passes out of one mouth, passes into a hundred ears.

Scholarship

964. The ink of the scholar is more sacred than the blood of the martyr.

Secret—Secrets

965. He only is secret who never was trusted.

966. Three may keep a secret if two of them are dead.

967. The sun discovers the filth under the white snow.

968. Tell nothing to thy friend which thy enemy may not know.

—Danish

969. A woman's idea of keeping a secret is to refuse to tell who told it to her.

970. The man who has no secrets from his wife either has no secrets or no wife.

971. When a secret is revealed, it is the fault of the man who confided it.

—French

972. Thy secret is thy prisoner; if thou let it go, thou art a prisoner to it.

—Hebrew

973. If you wish another to keep your secret, first keep it yourself.

—Latin

974. Give up the smallest part of a secret, and the rest is no longer in your power.

—German

Selectivity

975. Who gives to all denies all.

Self

976. What lies behind us and what lies before us are tiny matters compared to what lies within us.

Self-Appraisal

977. If you feel you have no faults, that makes another one.

978. Before a man can wake up and find himself famous he has to wake up and find himself.

979. When a man turns the light on others he must not expect to stay in the shade himself.

Self-Assurance

980. Believe in yourself and what others think won't disturb you.

Self-Confidence

981. He who knows little is confident in everything.

Self-Consciousness

982. He that has a great nose thinks everybody is speaking of it.

Self-Control

983. He conquers twice who conquers himself in victory.

—Latin

984. Government of the will is better than increase of knowledge.

985. The man who loses his head is usually the last one to miss it.

986. There is many a man whose tongue could govern multitudes, if he could only govern his tongue.

Self-Delusion

987. No man ever got himself out of trouble until he first admitted he was in trouble.

Self-Depreciation

988. He that makes himself dirt is trod on by the swine.

989. Who makes himself a sheep will be eaten by the wolves.

Self-Discipline

990. He overcomes a strong enemy who overcomes his own anger.

Self-Education

991. He that teaches himself has a fool for a master.

Self-Esteem

992. The minute you get the idea you're indispensable, you aren't.

Self-Gratification

993. You are best to yourself when you are good to others.

Self-Improvement

994. Sweep first before your own door, before you sweep the doorsteps of your neighbors.

—Swedish

Self-Interest

995. If I am not for myself, who will be for me.

Selfishness

996. No one has less to live for than one who lives only for himself.

997. He is a slave of the greatest slave, who serveth nothing but himself.

998. He that lives not somewhat in others, lives little to himself.
—Michel de Montaigne

999. No man is born unto himself alone;
Who lives unto himself, he lives to none.

Self-Judgment

1000. He who will have no judge but himself condemns himself.

Self-Justification

1001. He declares himself guilty who justifies himself before accusation.

Self-Knowledge

1002. Self-knowledge is the first step to the knowledge of God.

1003. What you think of yourself is much more important than what others think of you.

—Latin

1004. The first step to self-knowledge is self-distrust. Nor can we attain to any kind of knowledge, except by a like process.

Self-Love

1005. He that falls in love with himself, will have no rivals.

Self-Pity

1006. Self-pity is selfishness.

Self-Possession

1007. Possession is nine points of the law, and self-possession is the tenth.

Self-Praise

1008. Self-praise is half slander.

1009. Self-praise is no recommendation.

—Latin

1010. He is a fool that praises himself and a madman that speaks ill of himself.

—Danish

1011. Self-praise can be put in the same class as anything else you get for nothing.

1012. The trouble with singing one's own praises is that one seldom gets the right pitch.

1013. I always like to hear a man talk about himself because then I never hear anything but good.

Self-Punishment

1014. Nothing hurts more than the friendly letter that one never got around to writing.

Self-Respect

1015. Self-respect is the secure feeling that no one, as yet, is suspicious.

1016. These three are the marks of a Jew—a tender heart, self-respect, and charity.

—Hebrew

Self-Restraint

1017. He is twice a conqueror, who can restrain himself in time of victory.

1018. The person that always savs just what he thinks at last gets just what he deserves.

Self-Sacrifice

1019. Treasures in heaven are laid up only as treasures on earth are laid down.

1020. He who is ready to sacrifice himself, will not hesitate to sacrifice another.

1021. Self-preservation is the first law of nature, but self-sacrifice is the highest rule of grace.

Sentimentality

1022. Sentimentality is unearned emotion.

Sermon—Sermons

1023. The sermon you enjoy most is not likely to be the one that will do you the most good.

Service

1024. Unwilling service earns no thanks.

—Danish

1025. Service without reward is punishment.

1026. He that serves everybody is paid by nobody.

1027. They also serve who only stand and wait.

Shame

1028. Not to be ashamed of sin is to sin double.

—German

Sharing

1029. When someone shares his fears with you, share your courage with him.

1030. Of no worldly good can the joy be perfect, unless it is shared by a friend.

—Latin

Sickness

1031. Sickness shows us what we are.

—Latin

1032. Sickness comes on horseback, but goes away on foot.

Silence

1033. Silence brings friendship.

1034. Silence is often guilt instead of golden.

1035. Speech is oft repented, silence never.

—Danish

1036. When you have nothing to say, say nothing.

1037. Sometimes silence is not golden—just yellow.

1038. He who cannot keep silence cannot speak.

—Swedish

1039. To silence another, first be silent yourself.

—Latin

1040. Silence in the presence of evil is approval.

1041. Most of us know how to say nothing—few of us know when.

1042. Silence is the safest course, where a man distrusts himself.

1043. The silence of the people is a warning for the king.
—French

1044. Too many things that go without saying aren't left unsaid.

1045. Let a fool hold his tongue, and he will pass for a sage.
—Latin

1046. Do you wish people to think well of you? Don't speak.
—French

1047. He that speaks sows, and he that holds his peace gathers.

1048. He watches chess games in silence . . . What a superior man!
—Chinese

1049. Beware of a man that does not talk and a dog that does not bark.
—Portuguese

1050. What should not be heard by little ears, should not be said by big mouths.

1051. To speak wisely may not always be easy, but not to speak ill requires only silence.

1052. Silence is the best answer to the stupid.
The fool has his answer on the tip of his tongue.
—Arabian

1053. What is best for man? That he should possess intellect. If he lack intellect, then money whereby he will be respected. If he lack money, then a wife who will conceal his faults. If he lack a wife, then silence will hide his defects. And if he lack silence, then the best thing for him is the grave.
—Hebrew

Similarity—Similarities

1054. No two people are alike and they are both glad of it.

1055. No two children are alike, especially if one is yours and the other isn't.

Simplicity

1056. Nothing is more simple than greatness.

Sin—Sinner—Sinning

1057. Without knowledge there is no sin.

1058. A sin concealed is half pardoned.

—Italian

1059. Men are punished *by* their sins, not *for* them.

1060. With a good name one may easily sin.

—Dutch

1061. Only the wages of sin have no deductions.

1062. The greater the sinner, the greater the saint.

—English

1063. The Greek word for *wickedness* is *lawlessness.*

1064. Who is not ashamed of his sins, sins double.

—German

1065. Take away the motive, and the sin is taken away.

—Spanish

1066. The sin is not in the sinning, but in being found out.

1067. The sins ye do by two and two, ye must pay for, one by one.

Sincerity

1068. Sincerity and truth form the basis of every virtue.

Skill

1069. Try your skill in gilt first, then in gold.

—English

1070. Men are more important than tools. If you don't believe so, put a good tool in the hands of a poor workman.

Slander

1071. The truth is no slander.

1072. Mud thrown is ground lost.

1073. Tale-bearers are just as bad as the tale-makers.

1074. He who blackens others does not whiten himself.

—German

1075. If the ball do not stick to the wall, yet it will leave some mark.

1076. Slander slays three persons: the speaker, the spoken to, and the spoken of.

—Hebrew

1077. Slander cannot destroy an honest man ... when the flood recedes the rock is there.

—Chinese

Slavery

1078. The freedom of slaves is measured by the length of their chains.

Smallness

1079. Little pots soon boil over.

Smile—Smiles

1080. The smile that lights the face will also warm the heart.

Solitude

1081. Solitude is often the best society.

1082. If you can't stand solitude, perhaps you bore others too!

1083. The strongest man in the world is he who stands alone.

1084. They are never alone that are accompanied with noble thoughts.

Sorrow

1085. If sorrow would not talk it would die.

—Serbian-Croatian

1086. Sorrows remembered sweeten present joy.

1087. Sorrow is the child of too much joy.

—Chinese

1088. When the heart is full, the lips are silent.

1089. You cannot prevent the birds of sorrow from flying over your head, but you can prevent them from building nests in your hair.

—Chinese

1090. Sorrow for the death of a father lasts six months; sorrow for a mother, a year; sorrow for a wife, until another wife; sorrow for a son, for ever.

—Sanskrit

Soul

1091. The soul is not where it lives but where it loves.

Speech

1092. He that speaks much is much mistaken.

1093. Many speak much who cannot speak well.

1094. It is better to say nothing than not enough.

—Latin

1095. Discretion of speech is more than eloquence.

1096. Speech both conceals and reveals the thoughts of men.

—Latin

1097. He who says what he likes, hears what he does not like.

—Spanish

1098. The tongue is but three inches long, yet it can kill a man six feet high.

—Japanese

1099. I disapprove of what you say, but I will defend to death your right to say it.

—Voltaire

1100. The imprudent man reflects on what he has said; the wise man, on what he is going to say.

1101. When you have spoken the word, it reigns over you. When it is unspoken, you reign over it.

—Arabic

Spending

1102. Through not spending enough we spend too much.

—Spanish

Sportsmanship

1103. Everybody likes a good loser—provided it is the other team.

1104. It's harder to be a good winner than a good loser—one has less practice.

Stability

1105. Trees often transplanted seldom prosper.

—Arabian

1106. When you have both feet on the ground, you don't have far to fall.

1107. One way to keep a man's feet on the ground is to put a heavy responsibility on his shoulders.

Statesman—Statesmanship

1108. True statesmanship is the art of changing a nation from what it is into what it ought to be.

1109. Statesmanship is harder than politics. Politics is the art of getting along with people, whereas statesmanship is the art of getting along with politicians.

Stature

1110. A man never adds to his stature by treading on others' toes.

Steal—Stealing

1111. He who steals once is always a thief.

—Spanish

Stinginess

1112. A rich man who is stingy is the worst pauper.

—Yiddish

Straddling

1113. Straddling an issue is like straddling the middle of the road. You are likely to be hit from both sides.

1114. The enemies a man makes by taking a decided stand generally have more respect for him than the friends he makes by being on the fence.

Strength

1115. He who has great strength should use it lightly.

—Latin

Stubbornness

1116. A stubborn man doesn't hold opinions—they hold him.

Stupidity

1117. Genius has limitations; stupidity is boundless.

1118. Nature delights in punishing stupid people.

1119. Against stupidity the gods themselves contend in vain.

Submission

1120. Submission to one wrong brings on another.

—Latin

Success

1121. Success has many friends.

—Greek

1122. If at first you don't succeed, try a little ardor.

1123. When success turns a man's head he faces failure.

1124. Success comes in cans; failure in can'ts.

1125. Before you can score you must first have a goal.

—Greek

1126. It is not enough to aim. You must hit.

1127. Success is only a matter of luck—ask any man who fails.

1128. Worse than a quitter is the man who is afraid to begin.

1129. It signifies nothing to play well, if you lose.

1130. If you cannot win, make the one ahead break the record.

1131. To succeed, keep on doing what it took to get started.

1132. Success is getting what you want; happiness is wanting what you get.

1133. To know how to wait is the great secret of success.

—French

1134. It is a cart if it goes well, otherwise it is but timber.

—Hindustanian

1135. The dictionary is the only place where success comes before work.

1136. The secret of success is to do all you can without thought of fame.

1137. If at first you do succeed—it's probably your father's business.

1138. The best way to succeed in this world is to act on the advice you give to others.

1139. When your superior receives you as an equal, you are already his superior.

1140. Everybody's a self-made man, but only the successful ones are ever willing to admit it.

1141. Success is a ladder which cannot be climbed with your hands in your pockets.

1142. Success comes from having the proper aim as well as the right ammunition.

1143. The only difference between stumbling blocks and stepping stones is the way you use them.

1144. Some men succeed because they are destined to, but most men because they are determined to.

1145. Success comes to those who are neither afraid to fail nor discouraged by failures.

1146. The ladder of success must be set upon something solid before you can start to climb.

1147. Some think they have made a success of life, when all they've made is just a lot of money.

1148. The secret of financial success is to spend what you have left after saving, instead of saving what is left after spending.

1149. Big men become big by doing what they didn't want to do when they didn't want to do it.

1150. Probably the biggest advantage of success resides in the fact that you don't have to listen to good advice any more.

1151. The man who fails while trying to do good has more honor than he who succeeds by accident.

1152. The secret of success is to be able to make more money to meet obligations you wouldn't have had if you hadn't made so much money.

1153. A gauge of success is not whether you have a tough problem to solve, but whether it is the same problem you had last year.

Suffering

1154. He who suffers much will know much.

—Greek

1155. He who fears to suffer, suffers from fear.

—French

1156. Most people are quite happy to suffer in silence, if they are sure everybody knows they are doing it.

Suicide

1157. He dies twice who perishes by his own hand.

—Latin

1158. When all the blandishments of life are gone,
The coward sneaks to death, the brave live on.

—Martial

Superficiality

1159. A whitewashed crow soon shows black again.

—Chinese

Superiority

1160. A person who talks about his inferiors hasn't any.

Suspicion

1161. A man suspected is half condemned.

1162. Be ever vigilant, but never suspicious.

1163. At the gate where suspicion enters love goes out.

1164. Suspicion is a mental picture seen through an imaginary keyhole.

1165. Suspicion may be no fault, but showing it may be a great one.

1166. When you buy a vase cheap, look for the flaw; when a man offers favors, look for the motive.

—Japanese

1167. Avoid suspicion: when you're walking through
Your neighbor's melon patch, don't tie your shoe.

—Chinese

1168.
If you suspect him,
Then reject him.
If you select him,
Don't suspect him.

—Chinese

Swimming

1169. It's a good idea to begin at the bottom in everything except in learning to swim.

Sympathy

1170. No man limps because another is hurt.

—Danish

1171. Sympathy without relief is like mustard without beef.

T

Table-Turning

1172. Woe be to him whose advocate becomes his accuser.

Tact

1173. Tact is the knack of making a point without making an enemy.

1174. A foolish man tells a woman to stop talking, but a wise man tells her that her mouth is extremely beautiful when her lips are closed.

Talent

1175. To encourage talent is to create it.

1176. Great talents have some admirers, but few friends.

Tardiness

1177. People count up the faults of those who keep them waiting.

—French

1178. He that always thinks it is too soon is sure to come too late.

—German

Taste

1179. Good taste is the flower of good sense.

Tax—Taxes

1180. The reward for saving your money is being able to pay your taxes without borrowing.

1181. The tax? No wonder men abhor it!
    You raise a crop, they fine you for it!

—Chinese

Taxation

1182. Unnecessary taxation is unjust taxation.

1183. Any government big enough to give you everything you want is big enough to take everything you've got.

Teacher—Teachers—Teaching

1184. Who teaches, learns.

1185. Who is too old to learn is too old to teach.

1186. Good teachers cost more, but poor teachers cost most.

1187. Who teaches me for a day is my father for a lifetime.

—Chinese

1188. A good teacher is one whose ears get as much exercise as his mouth.

1189. A great teacher has always been measured by the number of his students who have surpassed him.

Temper

1190. He who loses his head is usually the last one to miss it.

1191. Too many people work up a head of steam before they find out what's cooking.

1192. Temper is a funny thing; it spoils children, ruins men, and strengthens steel.

Temptation

1193. An open door may tempt a saint.

1194. It is easier to stay out than get out.

1195. The less the temptation the greater the sin.

1196. All temptations are found either in hope or fear.
—English

1197. Everything tempts the man who fears temptation.
—French

1198. Every moment of resistance to temptation is a victory.

1199. The only way to handle temptation successfully is to yield to it.
—French

1200. If we avoid temptation, God will keep us from sinning.

1201. Don't worry about avoiding temptation—as you grow older it starts avoiding you.

1202. One can never know whether he is honest or not until he is really tempted.

1203. The only trouble with resisting temptation is that a man may not get another chance.

1204. Temptation wrings integrity even as the thumbscrew twists a man's fingers.
—Chinese

Thanksgiving Day

1205. Thanksgiving, to be truly Thanksgiving, is first thanks, then giving.

Theory—Theories

1206. Theory may raise a man's hopes but practice raises his income.

Thievery

1207. He who buys what he doesn't need steals from himself.

1208. A thief passes for a gentleman, when stealing has made him rich.

Thought—Thoughts

1209. If men would think more, they would act less.

1210. Think much, speak little, and write less.
—French

1211. Great thoughts reduced to practice become great acts.

Thrift

1212. Though you live near a forest, do not waste firewood.
—Chinese

1213. The best thing to save for your old age is yourself.

1214. A saver grows rich by seeming poor. A spender grows poor by seeming rich.

1215. No gain is so certain as that which proceeds from the economical use of what you already have.

—Latin

1216. If youth knew what age would crave,
It would both get and save.

Time

1217. Make use of time if you love eternity.

1218. By losing present time we lose all time.

1219. Why kill time when one can employ it?

—French

1220. The best way to kill time is to work it to death.

1221. Time wasted is existence, used is life.

1222. Money lost can be replaced but time lost is gone forever.

1223. People who have half an hour to spend usually spend it with someone who hasn't.

1224. Perhaps time also should come under the commandment, "Thou shalt not kill."

Time-Saving

1225. To save time is to lengthen life.

Timidity

1226. Who timidly requests invites refusal.

—Latin

1227. If you let everyone walk over you, you become a carpet.
—Bulgarian

Tolerance

1228. Deal with the faults of others as gently as with your own.
—Chinese

1229. It isn't necessary to blow out the other person's light to let your own shine.

1230. There are two sides to every question, because, when there are no longer two sides it ceases to be a question.

Traffic

1231. If you have plans for tomorrow, be careful today.

1232. It's better to be last in the traffic lane than first in the funeral procession.

1233. Do not depend on the other fellow because he may be depending upon you.

1234. If all the cars in America were placed end to end on a long hill, some fool would try to pass them.

Travel

1235. Travel only with thy equals or thy betters; if there are none, travel alone.

1236. To meet an old friend in a distant country is like the delight of rain after a long drought.
—Chinese

1237. He who would bring home the wealth of the Indies must carry the wealth of the Indies with him.
—Spanish

1238. When through foreign lands you stray,
Smile, and give the first "Good Day!"

—Chinese

Trickery

1239. Some people are so busy learning the tricks of the trade that they don't have time to learn the trade.

Trifle—Trifles

1240. Great floods flow from simple sources.

1241. The journey of a thousand miles begins with one pace.
—Chinese

1242. Small ills are the fountains
Of most of our groans.
Men trip not on mountains,
They stumble on stones.

—Chinese

Trouble—Troubles

1243. Trouble is to man what rust is to iron.
—Yiddish

1244. Trouble hunters are not always trouble shooters.

1245. Everyone shuns trouble unless it comes disguised as money.

1246. One trouble with trouble is that it usually starts out like fun.

1247. In trouble to be troubled is to have your trouble doubled.

1248. When we can't make light of our troubles, we can keep them dark.

1249. Trouble is often the lever in God's hands to raise us up to heaven.

Truth

1250. A half truth is a whole lie.

—Yiddish

1251. Children and fools tell the truth.

1252. Truth ill-timed is as bad as a lie.

—German

1253. When in doubt, tell the truth.

1254. Truth fears nothing but concealment.

—Latin

1255. Truth crushed to earth shall rise again.

1256. Withholding the truth suggests falsehood.

—Legal maxim

1257. Truth angers those whom it does not convince.

1258. Falsity binds and enslaves; truth makes men free.

1259. Beware of a half-truth; it may be the wrong half.

1260. Better suffer for truth than prosper by falsehood.

—Danish

1261. He that speaks truth must have one foot in the stirrup.

—Turkish

1262. When truth stands in your way it's time to change directions.

1263. Truth is the anvil which has worn out many a hammer.

1264. Truth has to change hands only a few times to become fiction.

1265. What is true by lamplight is not always true by sunlight.
—French

1266. Speak the truth sparingly unless you want to live the life of a hermit.

1267. A lie is a poor substitute for the truth, but the only one so far discovered.

Tyranny

1268. Resistance to tyrants is obedience to God.

1269. He who allows the oppression shares the crime.

U

Understanding

1270. What we do not understand we do not possess.

1271. The best way to be understood is to be understanding.

1272. Be not disturbed at being misunderstood; be disturbed rather at not being understanding.
—Chinese

Unhappiness

1273. Unhappiness is in not knowing what we want and killing ourselves to get it.

Uprightness

1274. If you stand straight do not fear a crooked shadow.
—Chinese

Usefulness

1275. What is useful cannot be base.

—Latin

1276. Greatness is a by-product of usefulness.

1277. Unless what we do is useful, glory is vain.

—Latin

1278. No life is pleasing to God that is not useful to man.

Uselessness

1279. What is the use of running, when you are on the wrong road?

V

Vacation

1280. The bigger the summer vacation the harder the fall.

1281. If you come home as happy as you leave, you have had a good vacation.

Value—Values

1282. Most folks pay too much for the things they get for nothing.

1283. We never know the worth of water until the well runs dry.

Vanity

1284. Human vanity being what it is, most people consider themselves exceptions to the rules.

Veracity

1285. A half-truth is the most cowardly of lies.

1286. Show me a liar and I will show you a thief.

1287. It is twice as hard to crush a half-truth as a whole lie.

1288. Liars begin by imposing upon others, but end by deceiving themselves.

Victory

1289. The greatest conqueror is he who overcomes the enemy without a blow.

—Chinese

Virtue

1290. Virtue is woman's honor; honor, man's virtue.

1291. Virtue may be overclouded for a while, but will shine at last.

1292. He who is virtuous is wise; and he who is wise is good; and he who is good is happy.

1293. Virtue practiced to be seen is not real virtue; vice which fears to be seen is real vice.

—Chinese

Vision

1294. You must scale the mountains if you would view the plain.

—Chinese

1295. A task without a vision is drudgery. A vision without a task is a dream. A task with a vision is victory.

W

War

1296. A just war is better than an unjust peace.

1297. There never was a good war nor a bad peace.

1298. One murder makes a villain, millions a hero.

1299. The fear of war is worse than war itself.
>   —Italian

1300. Even the lion has to defend himself against flies.
>   —German

1301. The war that will end war will not be fought with guns.

1302. A great war leaves a country with three armies—an army of cripples, an army of mourners, and an army of thieves.
>   —German

Waste

1303. Wilful waste brings woeful want.

Wealth

1304. He is rich who owes nothing.
He is poor who has nothing but money.

1305. Wealth is not his who hath it, but his who enjoys it.

1306. If money be not thy servant, it will be thy master.

1307. A great fortune in the hands of a fool is a great misfortune.

1308. A thief passes for a gentleman when stealing has made him rich.

1309. The greatest evidence of demoralization is the respect paid to wealth.

—French

1310. Covet wealth, and want it; don't, and luck will grant it.
—Chinese

1311. Some people think they are worth a lot of money because they have it.

1312. If you share a man's wealth, try to lessen his misfortune.
—Chinese

1313. Wealth conquered Rome after Rome had conquered the world.

—Italian

1314. If wealth can't bring happiness, it can often make misery a little more comfortable.

1315. Some people lose their health getting wealth and then lose the wealth regaining health.

Widowhood

1316. A buxom widow must be either married, buried, or shut up in a convent.

—Spanish

Wife—Wives

1317. All married women are not wives.

—Japanese

Willingness

1318. Those who wish to sing always find a song.

—Swedish

Wisdom

1319. A wise man changes his mind, a fool never.

1320. Wisdom is in the head and not in the beard.
—Swedish

1321. A man remains wise as long as he seeks wisdom. The minute he thinks he has found it, he becomes a fool.

1322. He alone is wise who can accommodate himself to all the contingencies of life; but the fool contends, and is struggling, like a swimmer, against the stream.
—Latin

Woman—Women

1323. Women in mischief are wiser than men.
—English

1324. Women resist in order to be conquered.
—Italian

1325. A truth-telling woman has few friends.
—Irish

1326. Women rouge that they may not blush.
—Italian

1327. To have the last word with a woman—apologize.

1328. A woman will never forgive a man if she is wrong.

1329. A woman either loves or hates; there is no third course.
—Latin

1330. A woman may suffer in many ways. But never in silence.

1331. A man thinks he knows, but a woman knows better.
—Chinese

1332. Men are the reason for women disliking one another.

—French

1333. The most praised woman is the one who is never spoken of.

—French

1334. Woman is like your shadow. Follow her, she flies; flee her, she follows.

—Chinese

1335. Ask a woman once or twice, and if she does not accept your view, take you hers.

—Irish

Words

1336. A round egg can be made square according to how you cut it; words would be harsh according to how you speak them.

—Japanese

Work

1337. Work as though you will live a hundred years; think as though you will die tomorrow.

—Bulgarian

Worry—Worries

1338. Worry grows lushly in the soil of indecision.

1339. Worry often gives a small thing a big shadow.

—Swedish

1340. Worry is interest paid on trouble before it falls due.

1341. Worry is today's mice nibbling on tomorrow's cheese.

1342. Never worry because the tide is going out. It always comes back.

1343. When we have nothing to worry about we are not doing much, and not doing much may supply us with plenty of future worries.

—Chinese

Worship

1344. He who carves the Buddha never worships him.

—Chinese

Y

Yielding

1345. Who does not go with you, go with him.

—Arabic

1346. The back is not broken by bending it.

—Amen-em-Apt, circa 700 B.C.

1347. The more you give in, the more you have to give in.

—Latin

1348. Yielding is sometimes the best way of succeeding.

—Italian

1349. It is being twice right to yield to one who is in the wrong.

1350. Be not the first man to quarrel, nor the last to make up.

Youth

1351. Youth lives on hope, old age on remembrance.

—French

1352. There would be miracles if youth could know and age could do.

—Bulgarian

1353. There is nothing wrong with the younger generation that the older generation didn't outgrow.

1354. The greatest disadvantage of young people today is that they have too many advantages.

1355. Blessed is the generation in which the old listen to the young; and doubly blessed is the generation in which the young listen to the old.

Z

Zeal

1356. Blind zeal can only do harm.

—German

1357. Zeal without knowledge is a fire without a light.

1358. Zeal is fit only for wise men but is found mostly in fools.

1359. Too much zeal is a bad soldier who fires before the word of command.